THE LAUGHING GAS AND OTHER POEMS

POETRY IS THE FREEDOM OF A POET
AS IS LAUGHTER TO A CHILD

DAVID T NICHOLAS

ISBN 979-888591931-9

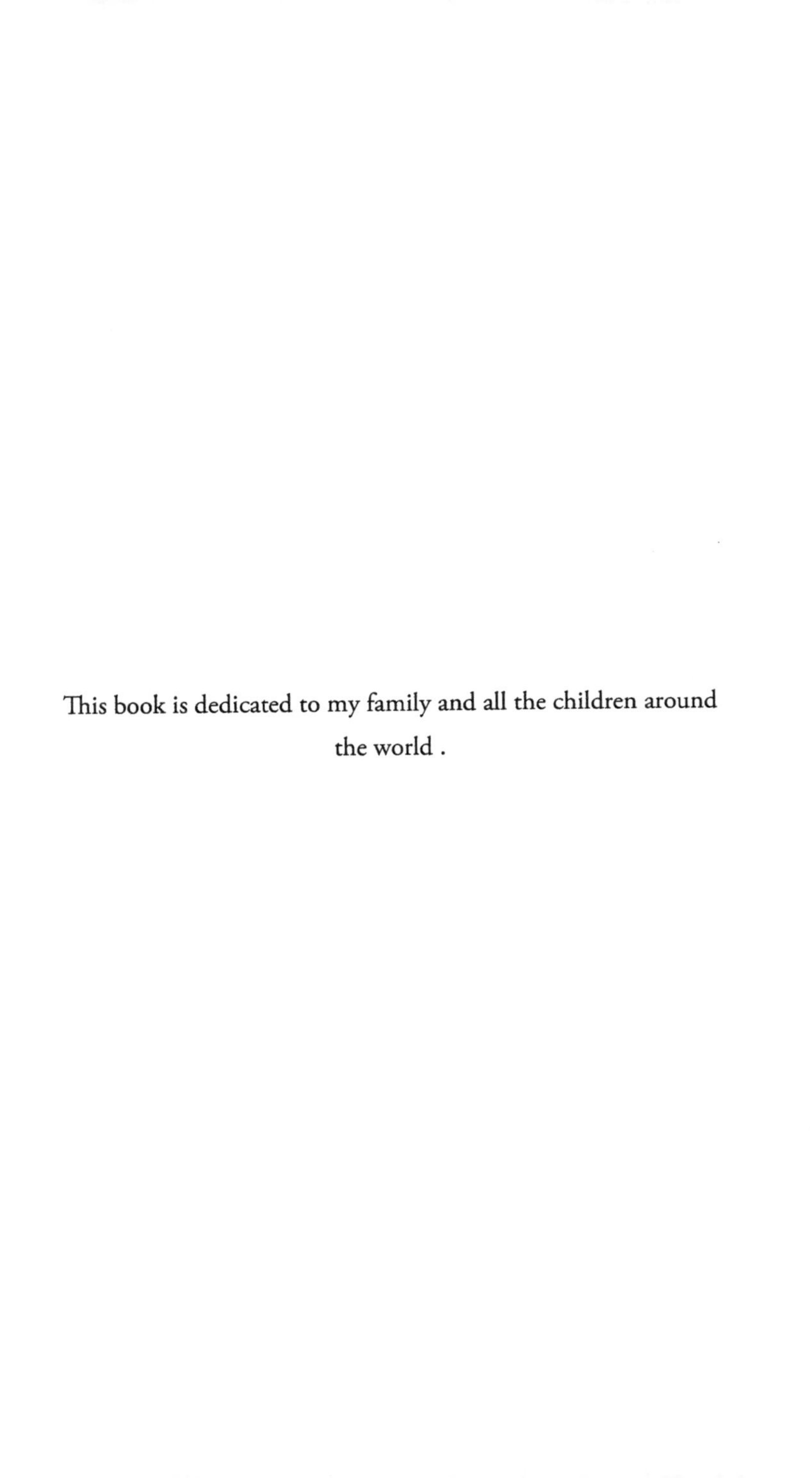

This book is dedicated to my family and all the children around the world .

Contents

Contents

1. Rainbow rainbow in the sky.

Rainbow rainbow in the sky
Thy appearance I know why
I even know for When and what.
So high up in the bright blue sky
Thy seven colours of thee underlie.
Thy colours remembered best
By the Word; VIBGYOR
A view so beautiful never seen
When the skies get clean
As that of a rainbow in the sky
Especially after some heavy showers
Every age Group says with joy
Rainbow rainbow in the sky.
What aren't you always in the sky?

2. This and That

A child's two words of tricks
When they are really at a fix

Or need something really quick
They know the words that would do the trick

I want this
I want that

I don't want this
I don't want that

Please get me this
please get me that

I wont eat this I'll eat that
I wont eat that I wont eat this

I only want that
I only want this

Oho the tantrums these words would play
some time for parents such a dismay.

A hundred way of saying this
And a hundred ways of saying that

Then he prays for this
And prays for that

Thanks God for this
And thanks for that

It's a child's favourite words
This and That .

3. The Night

The Night is dark and slient,
Full of brightness and whispers.
If one can hear the sounds of the night
Especially the ones that sound
Aloud and alarming during the day.
One would know what essence of magic
The night has brought to us
We talk but in whispers,
We walk but tippy toe ,
We see what we imagine; fear .
We pray more and forget less.
To remember the ones we love then
That's the real beauty of the night.

4. Happiness

Happiness is the perfect
key to life .
Happiness is everything
that one wishes for .
They wish it For themselves ,
Their family ,
Their loved ones ,
Their friends and neighbours,
Their country too
And everyone around them .
Those that wish upon it for others
Shall always have it in abduance
Because only when others
Are happy can one be happy .

5. laughing gas

I wondered what this really was
And how i got a bottle full.
I Opened the cap to take a look
It felt so good i began to smile and laugh ,
I took it wherever i went with me.
Where any who smelt, laughed with me.
I named it the laughing gas; as it made everyone laugh
In my heart i was so happy to make so many people laugh.
Guessed that the laughing gods must have created it
To make their work much easy on earth

Took it to school one day
Opened it in the most boring class
We laughed with the teacher till the end of day
It spread to the whole school
Oho what a hearty laugh the whole school had
In my heart i was so happy to make so many laugh in school

Then i went to my uncle's funeral
Still carried the bottle with me as i began to fall in love with it
I seen all weeping in tears and no life within.
I opened the bottle then
Just to see some life and no more tears
I guess first time a funeral was filled with life and laughter
A memorable funeral that will never be forgotten
Again in my heart i was so happy to make them laugh at a funeral.

Oho i guess i was the naughty type
To do such a thing everywhere
At last i looked upon the skies
And smiled and laughed at the gods above
Thanking them for the lovely creation 'The Laughing Gas'.

6. where the sounds all gone?

Snap you're fingers,
Clap you're hands,
Tap you're knees
and stomp you feet.
Now tell me where the sounds all gone ,
You can try it all , twice or thrice .
you'll still never know
where the sounds all gone?

7. My Dear Math

Doing Math wasn't fun
Most of the time I wanted to run.
Oho the numbers I learnt where everywhere
Even in my dreams to scare.
Addition was very easy I thought
Until the teacher taught me the carring plot.
Subtraction was easier than I thought
But the borrowing led to sorrowing alot .
Multiplying had a lot of tricks
Which I never got even after the stick.
Division was another term
Which had really alot to learn.
I finally began to get them all
Until word problems spooled them all .

Learning to me was always fun
Because I would always turn my back and run
Untill my mum caught me, and said;where you're going son
I always found a trick or two
Forgetting that it was learning too.
Playing was something I loved to do
Buy boy you're grounded was nothing new.
The homework I always had to do
Just imagine at late nights too.
The answers were right
But the method was wrong
In my mind they would all play like a horrible song
I always wondered what's wrong
For years I kept up with it all
And in my life it helped me overall.

8. The Air I breathe

Everyone has this in them
The air I breathe I care
The air my mom breathe I care
The air my dad breathe I care
The air my brother and sister breathe I care
The Air my loved ones breathe I care
The air others breathe I don't care
That just is really unfair
Keeping the air pure is a burden we all must bear
We must take a solemn oath and
say the air we breathe I really care
And promise to keep it pure and fair.

9. Family

Family may be a person ,
A place a thing or may be more
But one things for sure we know
that's its everything we know
Its someone we come to when we are lost
Its place no matter what we keep coming back
Its something more than memories
we treasure till our last breath

Its the only word where we can take all the adjectives.
Even if its wrong or right
its always corrected and made right
Weather its the morning, afternoon , evening or the night .

10. Love to play in clay

Children always love to play
If given a choice would mostly be clay
While playing , dirty will they always stay
Even in the bright sun's ray
would prefer that way till the skies turn grey
Seeing them parents are in a dismay
They literary don't know what to say
But: Seeing they children happy and smile
All their heart desires while
They love to play in clay
And won't mind doing it all day

11. Death (Cinquain)

Death
No more
Without life anymore
Now lost never found
Death

12. If you were nature

If you were nature
what would you be
Would you like to be a tree
Which is earth's life key
Would you be the huge mountains
Or the mountain ranges
Would you be the ocean or the seas
Would you be rivers , lake or a small pond .
Would you be a forest or the jungle
Or a beautiful garden .
Would you like to be the bright sun
Or the beautiful stars or moon at night
for nature so many a beautiful thing

i know its would hard to choose
There are many ways
That nature can be
What we would like to be
Or what we have to be
Is To be the one to take care of nature
Just like the way it provides and takes care of us.

13. The Country I Live in

The country I live in
Is the very country I would die for?
If called upon to confront death
Eye to eye and tooth for a tooth
I would stand tall and face
My enemies with courage and no fear.
The love for my country is something
That I cannot show
Or words can't express

Or my death wouldn't be enough
A country United as one
Is more than a billion people together
With a single soul within.

14. In my dreams

In my dreams
I could be the one I want to
In my dreams
I could go places that i want to
In my dreams
I can see people that i want to
in my dreams
I can hear things that i want to
in my Dreams
I can speak the words that i want to
There's more to life

in my dreams
Then then the real one I'm living in
the life in my dreams while i sleep
is the one i would always prefer
That the one in reality
But life has its owns ways
The ways of which you can live life
like how you live in you're dreams

15. Monkey on the roof top

Enter Caption

Monkey on the roof top
Sitting up there.
Why did you break in to my house?
When I was not there?
You Spared all the other rooms
But the kitchen you didn't spare.
You flipped all the leftover food
From the stove top.
You opened all the spice jars

And mixed them on the floor.
The fruits half eaten
And the vegetables untouched.
I see you ate what you like.
The kitchen is in a complete mess,
Oho now let me guess!
You flung around what you dislike.
I see you tried to put your head
into the flour, fell right into it
and tossed yourself out,
you with the container came tumbling down.
how risible you look now
with the spices all over you
smothered on top of the flour.
Now you look so funny
and that's something I'll remember.
Mr. Monkey on the roof top
Never come into my house
When I am not there.

16. Too much Too less

Too much is too bad
Too less is too bad
Too much is nada
Too much soon becomes Zilch
Too much should be abridged soon
Too much is belie with the soul
Too much obsession leads to depression
Too much depression leads to a malady
Too much malady eventually leads to death
Too much is too bad
Too less is to bad
So have enough; not too much , not to less

17. No greater Joy

No greater joy than seeing a seed
grow into a tiny little sappling
that you have planted
No greater joy than seeing
that tiny sappling you have grown
turn in a lovely plant
No greater than seeing the first bud
budding upon the plant
that you have planted
No greater than seeing the plant

maturing into a fine tree from
that plant you have planted
No greater joy than seeing that bud bloom
into a flower on the tree
that you have planted
No greater joy than to see that flower
turn into fruit upon the plant
that you have planted
burry a seed let it grow
and see the joy it will bring
in the seed that you have planted

18. Oho Gentle Sparrow

Oho gentle Sparrow
where are you now

when i was alittle
you were so many

I would often shoo you off
till there aren't any .

so small ,short tails ,stubby powerful beaks
you brought up love like that of aphorodite

I was so young never knew so
was always happy to see a Flutter of you

Now its only sorrowful to know
that there aren't many of you

In my heart i really wished
I never shooed the host of you

Oho gentle Sparrow
where are you now

19. Quibbering

Oho i was the quibbering type
I could do it day and night
especially if i knew i was right
coz an enemy will agree
And dear ones will agrue
but i always had to say aword or two
or have the last word for myself
sometime people would tell me shoo
In return i would tell them boo
the crazy faces i would make
would give the other person an ache
I could never walk away
from debating and making my point trite

like the one in front of me
untill i had the last word for myself

20. Darkness (Cinquain)

Darkness
No Light
Good over Evil
When we are blinded
Darkness

21. Do

If your Done doing what you do
Then do what you have to be get doing .

if you are doing what you have done
Stop and do something that has to be done .

Don't say you have done all youre work
because if you have really done ; then youre really done .

For in life you have to do alot
And there is alot of work for you and me to be done

We are really done ,
only when life is done with us .

22. Nature's Gentleness

The wind blows gentle breeze across the land.
The water flows gently through the valley's, lakes and rivers.
The ice melts gently from the mountain top
The fire blazes gently in the fire place
The molten lava from the volcanos gently cools down
The trees are gentle in their in their place .
So must we be as nature's gentleness
For we know what happens when
Nature isn't gentle anymore ?
So never put nature to the test
In the past history tells of nature's ravages.
So always be thankful for Nature's gentleness

23. Lost and Found

Finders keepers ,losers weepers
If you found something then you would be lucky
If you loose something you would be unlucky
If you found something and returned it
It's the same feeling you get
when you loose something and get it back .
if you find something that's not yours
try to return it to whosoever it belongs
and if you ever loose something don't weep
but try to look out for the one
who found your something
if something is lost it has to be found
and if something is found it had to be lost .
keep not what's yours, for if you do
you will loose both what is and what is not yours.

24. The beauty of a running Train at Night

Oho how beautiful is a running Train at Night.
With the random sight of burning lights
We see thru the window bright
Oho what a sight!

How musical is the sound of the running train at night.
Along with the wavy sounds of breeze.
Sometime gentle, sometime harsh.
You could even listen to a loud roar of the wind,
Oho what a sound!

And all as the train is trying to hustle.

Down towards your destination
Creating quiet a bustle.
I've experienced beauty in many ways
One of the most beautiful scene .
Is The beauty of a running Train at Night.

25. Each New Thought

Each new thought
Gives rise to a new hope.
Every second lost
Is hope that is lost.
Every thought that adds value to us
Is the little way in which we begin
To gain our hope back.
let not, the mind hold back
for when it does the thought
of hope is lost , open youre mind
and let out the hope of Each new thought.

26. Time heals all wounds

If you are physically hurt
And bear a temperament pain
That Cause strain and agony ,
Scars and disabilities may follow
Medicine may be temporary
But it's time and time alone
That will heal all wounds.
If you're mentally disquieted
You accept to be cured apace
For patience and undergone will Follow
To test you in your worst
Like there is no tomorrow
For you in this world
But just remember to
Pass each by being efficacious
As you believe and make others do
That time and time alone
Can heals all wounds.

27. A ball of life

Earth is a big ball of life
That belongs to life itself.
The Qualities of life are Brio
It will always restore itself
And make life possible
When it's feels there is threat
To life in itself.
One life leads to another.
One life depends on another.

And life alone can bring life.
That is the universal truth of life.
Life cannot be lifeless
Or exist in a lifeless entity
So, earth is big ball of life
So be viable when upon it .

28. Memories

If today is gone
It will never come back
But the memories
We make today
Can be the memories
We have for life
So make them count
Decide what are the memories
That you want to have
For the rest of your life.
Thee deeds that you do today
Irrespective good or bad
Will definitely come back to you
If you couldn't make a difference
In the world yesterday
Try to make it today
So you'll be remembered tomorrow
Life is collection of memories
Of yesterday and today for tomorrow
If you're wise you'll understand
If not , time will speak for itself.

29. Priceless

There are alot of things in this world
That are priceless to you and me
But there are things
That are priceless for everyone
A mother's love
A father's care
A protective brother
A sister's affection
The bond of friendship
The togetherness of a family
When you're loved one
Stands up for you against the world
The warmth of a blanket
The hand that feeds us
The early morning sun
The quiet and peaceful moon
A good day's work
A good night's sleep
God's blessings and love
And the thought
That God is watching us Always
These are really priceless
If you experienced it you will agree

There is no harm in you disagreeing
Because life is never the same For us all
we all have the right
To believe in what's priceless
For us and what's not .

30. Circle of Life

The circle of life
It has no beginning and end .
No one know how it began
No one knows how it will end.
But it's sure we know
All things good and bad about it.
What we should ,
And What we shouldn't
What we must ,
And what we mustn't.

We must know that there
Is nothing more precious and sacred
Than the circle of life.
It must be lived and passed on
For Eternity and sacrosanct
Is that of The circle of life .

31. Be yourself

Be happy for your happiness does count
But if you have no happiness within
Don't fake your emotions and hurt yourself
For you're sadness is at times
Happiness for many and vice - versa
It's always best to be your self
And learn to live with every emotion of life
Let others know who you are
By just being true to yourself
For the eyes believes in what it sees
For the ears believes in what it hears
And The tongue speaks of what it believes .
If one learns to live with all the emotions
Only then will they be able
to understand the emotions of others
So be yourself and carry you're
Emotions with you for it's only
You who truly knows what you're going thru.

32. If God is silent

If god is silent
Then what does it mean.
After all the prayers
And tears within
In silence I did it all .
Must I be loud and make noise ,
Shout and sing his name
For him to speak with me.
I know not the plans of God
I even desire not to
But would deeply want to know
After all that is happening on this Earth
And my life's Bereft.
If god is silent
Then what does it mean.

33. The Empty walls

The empty walls in the room
Speak no words
That's whom I am with
Most of the day
People aren't talking anymore
They are just smiling and waving away
No talking ,stand still and
most of the times walk away .
Can I compare them to
The empty walls in the room
Yes of course because
The world I am in they are the same to me
The empty walls that
Speak no words.

34. Sister

The one that you would miss the most
When not by your side is your sister of course
For if she's always by your side
She's definitely your worldly guide.

Someone whose always there
During your troubled time
Even if it's as Deep as a mine.
Her love that we can never measure
Just as the ocean that we treasure.

If life ever puts you down
In it she would never let you drown.
A mother's duty she always takes
When you're sick she always awakes.
Silent sacrifices she makes
No matter what ever it takes.

She'd never cry infront you
She knows it would break your heart too.
Her second thoughts are always you
You'd never believe that it's true.
So many little things for you she'd do
Which many a times is to bring a smile on you.

A love that a poems words can't express
But my love for her isn't any less.
Her name all of you can guess
Is your sister forever be blessed.

35. The Actor

We all are actors in our lives
Some with or without wives
Some for real
And some in reel
Some times with family and friends
Some times with enemies and strangers
You master every emotion
And become one you are not within
You hide you're real emotions
Taking a lot of precautions
we are born actors with emotions
inside us that are lager than the oceans
No one knows you're an actor in real
Unless you're one in reel

36. Brother

A person who forever would stand by eachother
Is none other than your brother .
With him you can fight
Even thou you're not right
But he always wishes to see your future bright
If ever you fear in the dark or the night
Just call on him and he'll always be by your sight
If you're ever in danger he'll hold you're hand tight
And for you till his last breath he would fight

You might want the world from him
But you truly are the world to him
If ever infront a tear should drop
His heart would surely tear apart
His love he can never express
Ther go as far as numbers excess .
If ever to choose the world or you
He'd definitely choose the one he loves that's you.
The bond that no one could ever tear apart
Even after life's depart

37. change my days

I wonder why god this to me;
He took my father and left my mother
Thou he knew i needed both.
Six sweet brothers and one beautiful sister
Having their own days and problems.

I asked god why he did this to me ,
I prayed and prayed the very way a saint would pray.
Even still, having a lot of bad days and problems in my life
I pray and pray ,give me a happy and peace full life.
All i ask god is to change my days and the days of my family
Looked around me and seen the problems around me
Everyone having their own days and problems.
Then i realize that i was selfish and not kind enough,
To help others or pray for others for better days and problems.
Solve the problems around you and your problems will be solved
All i ask god is to change my days and the days of the world around me.

38. Fear the Dark and not the day

Why do we fear the dark and not the day ?
When the day is filled
With more terrors than the dark
Imagine the worst that's happened to you
its all just happened mostly in the day .
The best things sometimes happens during the night
especially when we sleep and dream
can the day be peaceful like the night
Or can all the worries of day last
throughout the night
The night is peaceful and silent
causes less trouble and worry than the day
so why do we fear the dark and not the day ?

39. Difficult things to say

Some things are really difficult to say
As the things I say below
Weather the night is beautiful or the day
Is the sun more useful than the moon
Is life really better than afterlife
If love is a cure for all emotions
Or if laughter is really the best medicine
Is god always watching us
Does he really care about anyone
Living creature upon this Earth
Or is mankind left to fend for themselves
The surety of the beginning and end of life .
These are difficult things to say
You may or may not think my way
Maybe when you're wise enough
You know that these are things
That matter to us in life
And these are really difficult things to say .

40. Sugar and salt

Too much sugar
Too much salt
Spoils the lot .
Less sugar
Less salt
Makes the lot insipid.
Exact measure of sugar
Exact measure of salt
Pleases the lips
And the stomach too.
so one must learn to live life
like sugar and salt
In the exact measures

that our parents , siblings
loved and dear ones want us to be
especially live life in the measures
God wants us to live.

Printed by Libri Plureos GmbH in Hamburg, Germany